50 SHADES OF LOVE

A POETIC JOURNEY

HARSHIT KUMAR RAY

Made with ♥ on the Notion Press Platform
www.notionpress.com

Contents

Contents

Contents

Foreword

Hello there!

This book is a special journey into something we all know: love. Love is a big, wonderful feeling that makes our hearts feel warm and fuzzy. In this book, we follow the story of Veer and Vani, two people who experience love in many different ways.

Imagine each poem in this book as a little story, like pieces of a puzzle that fit together. These stories capture moments of love, from the very first glance to promises that last forever.

I wrote these poems to show how love can be exciting, sometimes a little bit sad, but always beautiful. I hope these words make you feel something special inside, something that reminds you of the love in your own life.

So, let's dive in together and explore the amazing journey of love through these simple and heartfelt words.

With warm wishes,

Harshit K. Ray

Preface

Dear Reader,

In the pages of "50 Shades of Love: A Poetic Journey," I invite you to step into a world where emotions cascade like a symphony, and every line is a heartbeat echoing with passion. This collection is not just a series of initials; it's a celebration of love in its purest, most visceral form.

Meet Veer and Vani – two souls whose love story dances through these verses. Their journey isn't just a tale of romance; it's a vibrant mosaic of emotions, a crescendo of laughter, and a profound exploration of what it means to truly, deeply love.

These poems are not just ink on paper; they are whispers of the heart, moments Šozen in time, and echoes of a love that refuses to be contained. They are the stolen glances, the unspoken words, and the silent promises that make love the most powerful force in the universe.

As you read, I encourage you to feel every word, let every line seep into your soul, and allow the magic of their love story to envelop you. This collection is more than poetry; it's a journey, an experience, and a reminder that love, in all its shades, is what makes us beautifully, unapologetically human.

In these initials, I've poured my heart and soul, hoping that you, dear reader, will find solace, inspiration, and perhaps see reflections of your own love story within these lines.

Acknowledgements

I want to take a moment to say thank you. This book, "50 Shades of Love: A Poetic Journey," wouldn't be possible without the support of some incredible people.

Firstly, to my family: your belief in us kept us going. Thank you for always standing by our side.

To my friends: your laughter and companionship inspired us. I'm grateful for the joy you brought into my life.

To all the writers and artists who inspired me: your creativity showed me what's possible. I'm in awe of your talent.

To you, my readers: your curiosity and open hearts mean the world to me. I hope these poems find a special place in your heart.

And finally, to the universe: thank you for the gift of creativity. I'm humbled by the endless possibilities you offer.

With heartfelt thanks,

Harshit Kumar Ray

1. Initials of Love

The First Glance

In a world bustling with faces,

Amidst the crowd's noisy traces,

There he stood, young and tall,

Caught in a moment's sudden fall.

Her eyes, like stars, shone bright,

In them, he found his guiding light.

A glance exchanged, a silent song,

Love's tender dance had just begun.

Heartbeats quickened, worlds collided,

In that gaze, love had decided,

To bind two souls, forever entwined,

A love story in the making, beautifully designed.

In the quiet of that fleeting look,

A universe of emotions, like an open book,

Hearts whispered secrets, pure and true,

In that first glance, love instantly grew.

And so, the tale of love commenced,

With a single look, hearts found sense,

In the language only lovers know,

Began a journey, destined to glow.

In Her Smile

In her smile, galaxies spun,

A universe of joy, second to none.

Her lips, curved in grace,

Painted the sky, a radiant space.

Eyes like oceans, deep and wide,

Held mysteries, none could hide.

In her smile, the sun found its light,

Chasing away the darkest night.

With every grin, the world would sway,

In the music of her laughter, they'd play.

Her smile, a beacon, a guiding song,

In its warmth, hearts would belong.

No words could match the tales it told,

Of love, of stories, both young and old.

In her smile, a universe unfurled,

A masterpiece, in a smile, a whole world.

Shared Laughter

Amidst life's hustle, they found delight,

In shared laughter, both day and night.

A language spoken without a word,

In giggles and chuckles, love was heard.

Echoes of joy in the air,

Moments of bliss, beyond compare.

Their laughter, a melody, sweet and clear,

Erasing worries, calming every fear.

In each other's eyes, they'd find the cue,

A shared joke, a moment to renew.

Hand in hand, hearts soaring high,

In shared laughter, love touched the sky.

For in those moments, they both knew,

In laughter shared, their love grew.

A bond unspoken, yet deeply felt,

In shared laughter, their hearts would melt.

Fateful Encounter

In a twist of fate, their paths aligned,

Two souls destined, intertwined.

A chance meeting, so brief and yet,

It sparked a fire they'd never forget.

A crowded street, a sudden glance,

Their hearts began a silent dance.

Time stood still, the world a haze,

In that moment, love found its ways.

Unseen forces brought them near,

In that fateful encounter, love was clear.

A touch, a smile, a shared breath,

Sealed their fate, defying death.

From that day on, life was new,

In each other's eyes, their world grew.

A fateful encounter, a love so grand,

In destiny's grip, they found love's strand.

The First Date

Nervous smiles, hearts aflutter,

On their first date, in a world of utter

Excitement and a bit of fear,

They embarked on a path sincere.

In a quaint café, under soft, warm light,

They shared stories in the quiet night.

His jokes made her laugh, her eyes, his muse,

On this date, love lit its fuse.

Awkward moments turned into grace,

As they lost themselves in each other's gaze.

Their laughter echoed, their hands found hold,

On this first date, a story of love was told.

A simple dinner, yet so much more,

A promise of love, they both swore.

In that moment, time seemed to freeze,

On their first date, love found its ease.

Moonlit Conversations

Beneath the tender glow of the moon,

They sat, two souls in sweet commune.

In the silence of the night so deep,

They shared secrets they vowed to keep.

Words flowed like a gentle stream,

In the moonlight, they dared to dream.

He spoke of stars, she of the sea,

In their conversations, love ran free.

Stories of childhood, dreams untold,

In the moonlit night, their hearts unfold.

They bared their souls under the celestial dome,

In those conversations, they found their home.

The moon witnessed vows, both fierce and kind,

In those whispers, their hearts aligned.

Under the night sky's ethereal gleam,

They found love in each other's moonlit dream.

Falling Slowly

A delicate dance, hearts in sync,

In love's web, they began to link.

Like autumn leaves, they fell so slow,

In the tender moments, love did grow.

His fingers brushed her hand with care,

In her eyes, he found a universe rare.

They fell, not in haste, but in sweet delay,

In each other's presence, come what may.

With every shared sigh and stolen glance,

They entered love's enchanting trance.

Falling slowly, like a gentle rain,

In love's embrace, they felt no pain.

Their love story, a melody composed,

In every falling leaf, love enclosed.

In this unhurried fall, they found their grace,

In the tender fall, they found their place.

Love's First Kiss

Underneath the silver stars so bright,

In the soft glow of the muted moonlight,

Their lips met in a lingering kiss,

A moment of bliss, of pure, sweet bliss.

His touch was gentle, her response divine,

In that kiss, they tasted love's sweet wine.

The world around them seemed to fade,

In love's first kiss, their worries laid.

A union of souls, a promise made,

In that kiss, a foundation laid.

Lips spoke what words could not express,

In love's first kiss, they found happiness.

A moment etched in memory, so fine,

In that kiss, love's stars aligned.

Their hearts now one, forever sealed,

In love's first kiss, a love revealed.

In Her Eyes

In her eyes, he found his universe,

A galaxy of love, tender and diverse.

Eyes like pools of endless grace,

Held his heart in a warm embrace.

Reflections of his dreams and fears,

In her eyes, he saw the passing years.

A silent language, unspoken but clear,

In her eyes, he found love sincere.

In every glance, a story told,

Of a love that would never grow old.

In her eyes, he found his truth,

A love that lasted from days of youth.

Her gaze, a beacon through joy and strife,

In her eyes, he found his life.

In those depths, love's secrets lie,

In her eyes, he saw the sky.

Love's Symphony

Amidst the quiet of the night,

Underneath the soft moonlight,

Their hearts began a gentle song,

A love that was sweet and strong.

His laughter was the melody bright,

Her smile, the harmonious light.

In every word and every touch,

They composed a love story, meant so much.

Together, they created a tune,

Underneath the golden, glowing moon.

Their love, a symphony of sweet sound,

In every note, their hearts were bound.

Through life's trials, through its glee,

They danced to love's sweet melody.

In every beat, in every rhyme,

They found love, pure and prime.

Their love story, a song so sweet,

In love's symphony, their hearts did beat.

A melody that forever played,

In love's music, they swayed.

2. Embracing the Journey

Weathering the Storm

In the heart of the tempest, they stood,

Hand in hand, like sturdy wood.

The storm raged with all its might,

But in their love, they found their light.

Raindrops fell, like tears from the sky,

Yet, in their love, they chose to fly.

Against the wind, they held their ground,

In love's shelter, they were safe and sound.

Thunder roared, lightning streaked the night,

But in their love, they found their might.

They weathered the storm, strong and brave,

In the face of chaos, love did save.

In the end, the storm did wane,

But in their love, there was no pain.

For storms may come, and storms may part,

But love, dear love, is where they start.

Healing Touch

In the silence of the darkest hour,

In the grasp of pain's relentless power,

Her touch was a soothing balm,

Healing wounds, bringing calm.

With a gentle hand, she wiped his tears,

Easing all his deepest fears.

Her touch, a magic, pure and true,

In her presence, his strength he drew.

In her touch, he found his peace,

His heart's ache, it did release.

Her hands, like angels, brought relief,

In her touch, he found his belief.

Her touch was more than mere skin,

It mended souls deep within.

In her touch, he found his way,

A healing touch, night or day.

Dancing in the Rain

Beneath the canvas of the cloudy night,

In the gentle drizzle's soft moonlight,

They danced, unburdened, hand in hand,

In raindrops, they found love so grand.

Laughter echoed in the pitter-patter,

Their dance, a love song that nothing could shatter.

In the rain's embrace, they found their cheer,

Drenched in love, they held each other near.

The world around them blurred and blurred,

In their dance, all worries were unheard.

In every twirl, in every spin,

They found a world of joy within.

No thunder could drown their happy song,

In the rain, they both belonged.

Dancing in the rain, a memory sweet,

In that moment, love found its beat.

Love's Fragrance

In the petals of a blooming rose,

In the scent that the soft wind chose,

Love found a way to make them swoon,

In the fragrance of a sweet monsoon.

Her perfume, like a love letter sent,

In its essence, their moments were lent.

A scent that lingered, a memory dear,

In love's fragrance, they drew near.

In the subtle notes of jasmine's grace,

They found love's tender embrace.

A fragrance that whispered tales of old,

In its aroma, their story was told.

Every flower, every whiff of the breeze,

Carried love in its fragrant tease.

In love's fragrance, they found their trace,

A scent that time could not erase.

In His Arms

In the circle of his warm embrace,

She found her sanctuary, her sacred place.

His arms, a fortress strong and true,

In their hold, her worries flew.

Against his chest, she heard his heart,

A rhythm that played its gentle part.

In his arms, she felt secure,

In their love, they found their cure.

His touch, a language they both knew,

In his arms, their troubles grew few.

With every hug, every tight hold,

In his arms, love was told.

In his embrace, she found her peace,

In his arms, love found its release.

A haven where all pain departs,

In his arms, she found her heart.

Stolen Moments

In the rush of life, amidst the crowd,

They found solace in silence, not loud.

Stolen moments, stolen glances,

In their love, life took its chances.

A stolen kiss in the morning light,

Underneath the blanket of the night.

Whispers shared in hushed tones,

In these stolen moments, love condones.

Hand in hand, they'd steal away,

In the quiet of the fading day.

In stolen moments, secrets told,

In their love, they found their gold.

In the midst of chaos, they'd find peace,

In stolen moments, love would increase.

These stolen moments, precious, few,

In them, love was raw and true.

Through Her Lens

Through the lens of her loving eyes,

He saw a world without disguise.

In her gaze, he found his worth,

A reflection of his soul's true birth.

She captured moments, both big and small,

In her photos, love would sprawl.

Through her lens, the world was bright,

In her vision, love took flight.

In every click, in every frame,

He saw their love, wild and tame.

Through her lens, their story told,

In pictures, love would unfold.

Through the colours, through the light,

Their love story took its flight.

In her lens, he found his truth,

A love immortalized, through her youth.

Love's Tapestry

In threads of gold and silver spun,

They wove a tale, two hearts as one.

Love's tapestry, intricate and grand,

In every stitch, their hearts were fanned.

With every laugh, with every tear,

They added hues, both far and near.

In love's tapestry, they found their art,

A masterpiece stitched from the heart.

Through storms they wove, and sunny days,

In love's tapestry, they found their ways.

Each challenge faced, each hurdle leaped,

In their love, the tapestry deepened and steeped.

A quilt of memories, both joy and pain,

In love's tapestry, they left a stain.

A tale of love, forever spun,

In threads of gold, their story begun.

Promise of Tomorrow

In the quiet of the evening's hush,

They made a vow, a sacred rush.

Hand in hand, under the twilight's gleam,

They promised forever, an endless dream.

With stars as witnesses, they declared,

A love so true, a bond so rare.

In whispered words, the promise made,

A commitment that would never fade.

To love in sickness, in health's bright light,

In every moment, both day and night.

They pledged their hearts, no matter what,

In that promise, love found its rut.

A promise of tomorrow, of days to be,

In their love, they found the key.

A commitment made under the moon's soft glow,

In that promise, love continued to grow.

The Proposal

Underneath the twinkling stars‘ soft gleam,

He knelt, his heart a hopeful dream.

A ring, a promise, in his trembling hand,

He asked her to walk life's endless sand.

With tears of joy and a whispered ’yes,'

She accepted, her heart in a happy mess.

In that moment, time seemed to freeze,

As they embarked on love's sweet tease.

The ring, a circle, no end, no start,

Symbolized their love, a work of art.

In the moonlight's gentle, tender kiss,

They sealed their fate, in wedded bliss.

A proposal made, a future bright,

In that moment, their love took flight.

Hand in hand, they faced tomorrow's sun,

In the promise of forever, two hearts became one.

3. Building A Forever

The Engagement Ring

A glittering promise on her hand,

An engagement ring, a love so grand.

In its sparkle, their future gleamed,

In her eyes, he found his dream.

A diamond's glow, a love so true,

In the ring, their vows they drew.

It shone like their smiles, bright and clear,

In the ring, their love was near.

With every glance at that precious thing,

They felt the joy that love could bring.

In the circle, unending and strong,

They found where they truly belong.

An engagement ring, a symbol so bright,

In its sparkle, they found their light.

A promise made, in that tiny band,

A love story, forever planned.

Family Blessings

In the circle of family, love did bloom,

In their blessings, there was no room for gloom.

Parents' smiles, siblings' cheer,

In family's love, they held dear.

In every hug, in every touch,

They felt love's blessings, oh so much.

Grandparents' wisdom, children's glee,

In family, love flowed endlessly.

Their union celebrated, their love embraced,

In family's warmth, they found their place.

Aunts, uncles, cousins, and more,

In family's love, they found the core.

In family gatherings, laughter and song,

In their midst, love was strong.

In family, they found a treasure,

A love that gave without measure.

Building a Home

With every brick laid, love did grow,

In their home, love's rhythm did flow.

In the walls, in the floors, in the ceiling high,

Love echoed in every sigh.

With paint and passion, they adorned,

In every room, their love was sworn.

A home built not just with bricks and wood,

But with promises made, both pure and good.

In the kitchen, love found its taste,

In the garden, love embraced the space.

Every corner, every cozy chair,

In their home, love was always there.

With every story shared, every tear shed,

In their home, love was deeply bred.

A sanctuary of joy, of laughter, of grace,

In their home, love found its place.

Love's Recipe

In the kitchen's aromatic embrace,

They found love in every taste.

A pinch of laughter, a spoonful of care,

In love's recipe, they became a pair.

In the sizzle of spices, love did dwell,

In every dish, love's tale it would tell.

Cooking together, side by side,

In shared moments, love did reside.

Ingredients of patience, of understanding sweet,

In love's recipe, they found their beat.

With every recipe, with every dish,

They found love, a fulfilling wish.

In the kitchen's warmth, love did brew,

In pots and pans, their love grew true.

A recipe of love, both tried and tested,

In their culinary love, they felt blessed.

The Wedding Dress

In lace and silk, dreams took flight,

A wedding dress, pure and white.

In its folds, hopes and wishes sewn,

A symbol of love, both theirs and known.

With every stitch, every tiny bead,

In the wedding dress, love took the lead.

A train of dreams, a veil so sheer,

In the dress, love's presence clear.

As she wore it, a princess bride,

In the wedding dress, love stood beside.

A gown of promises, of future bright,

In its elegance, their love took flight.

In the wedding dress, she found grace,

In its beauty, love found its place.

A garment woven with love's finesse,

In the wedding dress, they found happiness.

Eternal Vows

In the presence of friends and family dear,

They stood, hearts filled with love and fear.

With trembling voices, vows they'd share,

In those words, love was laid bare.

"To have and to hold," they softly said,

In those vows, love's path they tread.

"For better or worse," their promise strong,

In those vows, they did belong.

In sickness and health, till death do part,

In those words, they pledged their heart.

A promise made, forever true,

In those vows, their love anew.

With rings exchanged, a circle complete,

In those vows, their love was replete.

Eternal vows, in whispers blessed,

In those promises, they found their rest.

The Wedding Day

Underneath the azure sky so vast,

Their wedding day had come at last.

In the air, a sense of sweet perfume,

Love was the bride, the groom.

In the church, in hushed delight,

They exchanged vows, their love in sight.

Her dress, a vision, in the morning light,

In his eyes, she was pure and bright.

With every step down the aisle, so slow,

In love's glory, they began to grow.

Hand in hand, hearts intertwined,

In their union, love defined.

With blessings whispered, with prayers said,

In their hearts, love's banner spread.

In that moment, under the arch so grand,

In their wedding day, love took its stand.

In the laughter shared, in the tears shed,

In their wedding day, love was spread.

A promise made, in joy they'd sway,

In their wedding day, love found its way.

First Dance

In the soft glow of the twinkling lights,

They took the floor on that magical night.

His hand in hers, her head on his chest,

They swayed to the music, love at its best.

In the melody's embrace, they found their song,

In each other's arms, they both belonged.

With every step, with every beat,

They danced in love, both swift and sweet.

Her dress swirled like a silken dream,

In his eyes, she was his heart's own theme.

With every twirl, love found its place,

In their first dance, they embraced grace.

Underneath the stars, they danced away,

In the music, love had its say.

Their first dance, a memory divine,

In that moment, their love did shine.

Midnight Serenade

Under the velvet curtain of the midnight sky,

He strummed his guitar, stars as witnesses high.

In the hush of the night, his voice took flight,

A serenade to her, in the stillness of the night.

Moonbeams danced in her sleepy eyes,

As he sang, beneath the silent skies.

His love, a melody, in the quietude so deep,

In his serenade, her heart did leap.

With every note, with every tune,

In the midnight serenade, love did swoon.

His words, like whispers, reached her soul,

In the serenade, love found its goal.

A lullaby of love, in the midnight's glow,

In his serenade, emotions did flow.

Underneath the stars, in the serenade so rare,

Love sang to her, in the midnight air.

Love's Journey

Hand in hand, they walked the shore,

Love's journey, an open door.

Footprints left in sands of time,

In love's journey, they found their rhyme.

Through valleys low and mountains high,

In love's journey, they reached for the sky.

In every trial, in every test,

Love's journey was their very best.

With every sunrise, with every night,

In love's journey, they found the light.

In laughter shared and tears they wept,

Love's journey, a secret well kept.

In every chapter, in every page,

Love's journey, a lifetime stage.

Through every twist, through every turn,

Love's journey, forever to burn.

Hand in hand, they faced the unknown,

In love's journey, their hearts had grown.

A tale of love, both wild and free,

In love's journey, they found eternity.

4. Bearing The Depths

Homecoming

In the quiet hush of the evening's glow,

He returned home, his heart in a warm flow.

She stood there, a smile upon her face,

In her embrace, he found his place.

After days apart, in distant lands,

He felt the touch of her loving hands.

Homecoming, a melody, in their hearts did play,

In that moment, worries washed away.

She cooked his favourite meal with care,

In the homecoming, love filled the air.

Familiar scents, a comforting sight,

In their home, love found its light.

In the stories shared, in the laughter loud,

In the homecoming, they felt so proud.

Hand in hand, under the evening star's dome,

In the homecoming, they found their home.

Love's Sanctuary

In the heart of their shared abode,

They found more than bricks and roads.

A sanctuary, love's quiet place,

In each other's arms, they found grace.

In the walls that heard their laughter ring,

In the rooms where they learned to sing,

Love's sanctuary, where worries cease,

In its embrace, they found their peace.

A haven where dreams took flight,

In love's sanctuary, they found light.

In every whisper, in every prayer,

Love's sanctuary was always there.

With every tear, with every smile,

In love's sanctuary, they found their aisle.

A place where scars would fade,

In love's sanctuary, memories made.

In love's sanctuary, they both knew,

Their love would always hold true.

A sanctuary not just made of stone,

In love's sanctuary, they found their own.

In His Words

In the quiet of the twilight's haze,

He spoke his heart in myriad ways.

In his words, love found its prose,

A story told in verse, in rhyme, in throes.

With every whisper, with every sigh,

In his words, love soared high.

He painted love in colours bright,

In his words, she found her light.

In his phrases, she found her song,

In his words, she felt so strong.

He spoke of love, both fierce and kind,

In his words, peace of mind.

In every letter, in every line,

In his words, love was so divine.

His voice, a melody, sweet and clear,

In his words, she held love near.

In the echo of his soft refrain,

In his words, love had no chain.

A language that only lovers knew,

In his words, their love true.

Love's Legacy

In the tapestry of time, they wove,

A legacy of pure, unending love.

Through trials faced and battles won,

In love's legacy, their story spun.

In the laughter shared, in tears they shed,

In love's legacy, their path was led.

A tale of love, both deep and wide,

In love's legacy, they took pride.

Their children's eyes, their laughter sweet,

In love's legacy, their love did repeat.

Lessons taught, both gentle and wise,

In love's legacy, they found their ties.

Grandchildren's giggles, their innocence pure,

In love's legacy, their love would endure.

A family bound by love's soft thread,

In love's legacy, they found their stead.

The Unspoken Words

In the silence of their shared gaze,

Lay a story, beyond words' maze.

In the unspoken words, love would dwell,

In glances exchanged, in tales they'd tell.

Eyes met eyes, a language unknown,

In the unspoken words, love had grown.

In a touch, a brush, a fleeting smile,

In the unspoken words, love would compile.

In every sigh, in every breath,

In the unspoken words, love found its depth.

In the night's calm and day's bright light,

In the unspoken words, love took flight.

In the quietude of the breaking dawn,

In the unspoken words, their love was drawn.

A language that only hearts could hear,

In the unspoken words, love was near.

In the unspoken words, a universe found,

In silence, their love made no sound.

A love story, in whispers heard,

In the unspoken words, love occurred.

Love's Harvest

In the fields of their shared endeavour,

They reaped the fruits of love, and never

Did they imagine such a bounteous yield,

In love's harvest, a fertile field.

With every smile, with every tear,

In love's harvest, they felt it clear.

Seeds of kindness, of patience sown,

In love's harvest, their hearts were known.

With each sunrise and every night,

In love's harvest, they found delight.

The yield of trust, the crop of care,

In love's harvest, they laid it bare.

In the orchard of their endless affection,

In love's harvest, they found direction.

Harvesting joy and harvesting peace,

In love's harvest, their love did increase.

Love's harvest, a plentiful array,

In their hearts, it found a way.

A crop of love, both wild and sweet,

In love's harvest, they found their seat.

The Anniversary

In the quiet of their shared space,

They celebrated years of grace.

An anniversary, marked in time,

In their hearts, love's sweetest chime.

With every passing year, they grew,

In love's garden, their bond true.

Anniversary candles, aglow so bright,

In their love, they found the light.

Hand in hand, they'd walked the years,

Through joys and sorrows, through hopes and fears.

In the anniversary's tender embrace,

They found the beauty of love's grace.

Memories woven, both old and new,

In their anniversary, love renewed.

In every kiss, in every smile,

They celebrated love, mile by mile.

With every year, their love did bloom,

In the anniversary, they found no gloom.

A love story written in time's grand story,

In their anniversary, they found their glory.

Love's Reflection

In the stillness of the tranquil lake,

They saw their love, a gentle ache.

Reflections danced upon the water's face,

In love's reflection, they found their place.

Their smiles mirrored in the ripples' song,

In love's reflection, they both belonged.

In every glance, in every touch,

Love's reflection meant so much.

As the sun dipped low, and stars took flight,

In love's reflection, they found their light.

Their shadows merged, becoming one,

In love's reflection, their journey spun.

In the water's mirror, they saw their truth,

In love's reflection, the fountain of youth.

A reflection of a love so deep,

In love's reflection, their hearts did leap.

In the silent lake, love found its way,

In love's reflection, they both would stay.

A love story, on water's gentle complexion,

In love's reflection, their eternal connection.

Beyond the Stars

Beyond the stars, where dreams take flight,

They found a love, pure and bright.

In the cosmic expanse, they felt so small,

Yet their love, it touched them all.

Through galaxies vast and nebulas grand,

They wandered, hand in hand.

In the universe's vast embrace,

They found their own tranquil space.

Beyond the stars, where time does flee,

They found a love, just meant to be.

In constellations, their story was drawn,

In love's cosmic dance, they were drawn.

Through black holes and supernovas bright,

In love's realm, they took flight.

Beyond the stars, where infinity lies,

They found a love that never dies.

In the cosmic whispers, in the quiet night,

They found love's eternal light.

Beyond the stars, where all ends and starts,

They found a love that fills all hearts.

Love's Symphony Continues

In every beat, in every refrain,

Love's symphony played, relieving pain.

With each note, their hearts did swell,

In love's symphony, they found it well.

A crescendo of joy, a soft, sweet tune,

In love's symphony, they danced under the moon.

Harmony woven in every chord,

In love's symphony, they found their Lord.

In minor keys and notes so high,

In love's symphony, they touched the sky.

Melodies that whispered, harmonies grand,

In love's symphony, they found their band.

With violins weeping, and trumpets blare,

In love's symphony, they found solace there.

Through life's discord, and times of ease,

In love's symphony, they found their peace.

A timeless song, forever in bloom,

In love's symphony, they found no room for gloom.

Through every trial, every song, every verse,

In love's symphony, they found love, diverse.

5. Bonds Beyond Words

Love Letters

In ink and paper, emotions poured,

Love letters, their hearts' accord.

Each word penned with tender care,

In love letters, their souls laid bare.

Pages filled with love's sweet prose,

In love letters, their affection arose.

Words like petals, soft and true,

In love letters, their feelings grew.

With every stroke of the pen, they'd say,

In love letters, they found their way.

Expressions of love, both fierce and kind,

In love letters, their hearts entwined.

Sealed with kisses, scented with dreams,

In love letters, love's vast streams.

Through distance, through time apart,

In love letters, they shared their heart.

In every letter, love's story was told,

In love letters, their hearts did fold.

A chronicle of love, both near and far,

In love letters, they found who they are.

Sunset Serenity

In the amber glow of the setting sun,

They found a peace, a love just begun.

The sky painted in hues of gold and red,

In sunset serenity, they found their bed.

Hand in hand, they'd watch the day retire,

In the quiet of the evening's fire.

In the fading light, love softly spoke,

In sunset serenity, their spirits awoke.

The world turned silent, the birds took flight,

In sunset serenity, they felt the night.

A moment suspended, time seemed to cease,

In the tranquil evening, they found their peace.

As the sun dipped low, painting the sky,

In sunset serenity, they found the why.

A love story written in the evening's hue,

In sunset serenity, their love grew true.

In the quiet of the fading light,

In sunset serenity, they found their flight.

A moment, a memory, in the day's descent,

In sunset serenity, their hearts content.

The Shared Bookshelf

In the corner of their cozy abode,

Stood a bookshelf, a love story it told.

Each book a chapter, each tome a tale,

In the shared bookshelf, love would prevail.

From classics old to stories new,

In the shared bookshelf, their love grew.

Pages turned, words softly read,

In the shared bookshelf, they found what's unsaid.

His favourites stood next to her best,

In the shared bookshelf, love was confessed.

Mysteries, romances, adventures wide,

In the shared bookshelf, their worlds did collide.

In whispered discussions late at night,

In the shared bookshelf, they found their light.

A literary journey, both vast and grand,

In the shared bookshelf, they found their land.

With every book, a memory made,

In the shared bookshelf, love stayed.

A collection of stories, both fiction and real,

In the shared bookshelf, they found their zeal.

In the wisdom of authors, in characters bold,

In the shared bookshelf, their love took hold.

A testament written, both simple and profound,

In the shared bookshelf, their love knew no bound.

Love's Canvas

On the canvas of their shared dreams,

They painted love in countless streams.

Brushstrokes of passion, colours bright,

In love's canvas, they found their light.

In every smile, in every tear,

Love's canvas held memories dear.

Bold strokes of laughter, gentle hues of care,

In love's canvas, they found a rare flare.

With every touch, their love would blend,

In love's canvas, they'd make amends.

Splashes of affection, strokes so tender,

In love's canvas, their hearts did render.

In the masterpiece of love they'd weave,

In love's canvas, they found reprieve.

A work of art, both vivid and grand,

In love's canvas, they'd understand.

On this canvas, they etched their story,

In love's canvas, they found their glory.

A painting of love, both vibrant and vast,

In love's canvas, they found their cast.

The Little Things

In the touch of morning sunlight's kiss,

In the warmth of shared blankets' bliss.

In whispered secrets late at night,

In love's little things, they found their light.

A stolen glance, a secret smile,

In the little things, they walked that mile.

In cups of tea and morning talks,

In love's little things, they found no mocks.

A handwritten note, a surprise treat,

In the little things, love was sweet.

In comforting words, in soothing sighs,

In love's little things, they found the skies.

In every gesture, both big and small,

In the little things, they gave their all.

In silent moments, in words unspoken,

In love's little things, their hearts were woven.

In shared jokes and quiet laughter,

In the little things, they found their after.

In love's little things, forever they'd cling,

For in those moments, they found everything.

Love's Resilience

In the face of storms, in the darkest night,

Love stood strong, a guiding light.

Through trials fierce and tempests wild,

Love's resilience was undefiled.

With every tear, with every ache,

Love's resilience refused to break.

In the face of sorrow, it stood tall,

Love's resilience conquered all.

Like a tree, its roots deep in the earth,

Love's resilience found its worth.

In adversity, it learned to bend,

But it never broke, it never waned.

In love's resilience, they found their might,

In the fiercest storm, in the harshest fight.

A love unyielding, both fierce and true,

In love's resilience, they grew anew.

With every challenge, love found its way,

In love's resilience, they held dismay at bay.

A love story, not just of joy and bliss,

But of love's resilience, its enduring kiss.

Morning Bliss

In the soft caress of the morning light,

They found a love, pure and bright.

The sun painted the sky in hues of gold,

In morning bliss, their love story told.

With sleepy eyes and tangled hair,

In morning bliss, they found solace there.

Whispers shared 'neath the waking sun,

In morning bliss, love had begun.

Breakfasts made and coffee sipped,

In morning bliss, their spirits flipped.

A new day dawned, a fresh start,

In morning bliss, they found their heart.

In the shared silence, in the softest kiss,

In morning bliss, they found their bliss.

A love that grew with the rising sun,

In morning bliss, two hearts became one.

Love's Echo

In the quiet of the midnight air,

Love's echo whispered, soft and rare.

It reverberated through silent halls,

In love's echo, they heard love's calls.

With every beat of their hearts in sync,

In love's echo, they found their link.

Through spaces vast, both near and far,

In love's echo, they found where they are.

In laughter shared, in tears they shed,

In love's echo, their love was spread.

It echoed through mountains, across the sea,

In love's echo, their souls danced free.

In the echoes of their whispered words,

In love's echo, their hearts took flights like birds.

A resonance that time couldn't erase,

In love's echo, they found their place.

In the quietest moments, in the loudest cheer,

In love's echo, they held love near.

A symphony of love, both soft and loud,

In love's echo, their love was proud.

Love's Lullaby

In the cradle of the crescent moon,

They found a love, a tender tune.

In love's lullaby, the night would sing,

A melody where their hearts took wing.

Underneath the quilt of stardust bright,

In love's lullaby, they'd say goodnight.

Whispers soft, like the rustle of leaves,

In love's lullaby, they found reprieves.

In the quiet hum of the night's soft song,

In love's lullaby, they'd both belong.

A soothing rhythm, both gentle and kind,

In love's lullaby, peace they'd find.

With every note, with every sigh,

In love's lullaby, they'd soar high.

A melody of love, both soft and grand,

In love's lullaby, they'd understand.

In the hush of night, love would stay,

In love's lullaby, they'd dream away.

A lullaby of love, so sweet,

In love's lullaby, their hearts would meet.

The Everlasting Promise

Under the vast canvas of the sky,

They made a promise, neither would deny.

An everlasting vow, pure and true,

In that moment, their love they knew.

With stars as witnesses, they did declare,

An everlasting promise, a love so rare.

To stand by each other, come what may,

In the light of the sun or the moon's soft ray.

Through trials and joys, through laughter and tears,

In their everlasting promise, they'd conquer fears.

Hand in hand, they'd face each day,

In their everlasting promise, come what may.

In sickness and health, in joy and strife,

In their everlasting promise, they'd embrace life.

To cherish and love, till the end of days,

In their everlasting promise, love would always blaze.

A commitment made, in the quiet of night,

In their everlasting promise, they found their light.

A love story written in stars above,

In their everlasting promise, they found endless love.

end Note

In the closing chapter of this book, we've traversed the depths of love's myriad shades, Šom the first blush of affection to the quietude of lasting commitment. Each poem etched a Šagment of a timeless tale, woven with threads of passion, resilience, and joy. But as the final page turns, it's not the end but a pause in this love story. Love, after all, is boundless and ever-evolving, and so is the story of Alex and Jenniffer. As we bid adieu to this volume, we leave you with a whispered promise: there's more to come. Part 2 awaits, where their journey continues, unveiling new chapters of their life together, with Šesh poems, new challenges, and enduring love. Thank you for being a part of this poetic odyssey. Stay tuned for the next volume, where love's saga will find its voice once more, and the tale of Alex and Jenniffer will dance in the verses again. Until then, let the echoes of these poems remind you that love, in all its forms, is a story that never truly ends.

www.ingramcontent.com/pod-product-compliance
Lightning Source LLC
La Vergne TN
LVHW041110150826
845673LV00007B/1993

* 9 7 9 8 8 9 1 8 6 1 6 8 8 *